★★★★★
MLB TEAMS

St. Louis CARDINALS

KENNY ABDO

Fly!
An Imprint of Abdo Zoom
abdobooks.com

abdobooks.com

Published by Abdo Zoom, a division of ABDO, P.O. Box 398166, Minneapolis, Minnesota 55439.

Printed in the United States of America, North Mankato, Minnesota.
102025
012026

Photo Credits: AP Images, Getty Images, Icon Sportswire, Shutterstock
Production Contributors: Kenny Abdo, Jennie Forsberg, Grace Hansen
Design Contributors: Candice Keimig, Neil Klinepier

Library of Congress Control Number: 2025936810

Publisher's Cataloging-in-Publication Data

Names: Abdo, Kenny, author.
Title: St. Louis Cardinals / by Kenny Abdo
Description: Minneapolis, Minnesota : Abdo Zoom, 2026 | Series: MLB teams | Includes online resources and index.
Identifiers: ISBN 9798384940333 (lib. bdg.) | ISBN 9798384941095 (ebook) | ISBN 9798384941477 (read-to-me ebook)
Subjects: LCSH: St. Louis Cardinals (Baseball team)--Juvenile literature. | Baseball teams--Juvenile literature. | Professional sports--Juvenile literature. | Sports franchises--Juvenile literature. | Major League Baseball (Organization)--Juvenile literature.
Classification: DDC 796.357--dc23

Table of CONTENTS

CARDINALS

With sharp players and sky-high skills, the Cardinals rattle rivals' cages and keep St. Louis, Missouri, buzzing with excitement for baseball!

With a nest full of Hall of Famers, World Series wins, and big-league **records**, the Cardinals have built a **legacy** that soars high over Mound City!

WORLD CHAMPIONS
DRAFT KINGS
OVERALL MLB LEADERS
TODAY'S FANTASY POINTS
2B Brad Miller 36.0
3B Brad Miller 36.0
P Lance Lynn 32.7
1B Paul Goldschmidt 31.0
OF George Springer 31.0
2019
NL CENTRAL DIVISION
CHAMPIONS
STIFEL
ESTATE PLANNING
SSMHealth
ST. LOUIS POST-DISPATCH
Cardinals 48
WIETERS 32
Cardinals 23

BATTER UP!

The team traces its roots back to 1882, when a team called the St. Louis Brown Stockings began playing in the American Association. The team later shortened its name to the Browns and joined the **National League** (**NL**). Finally, in 1900, the team's nickname became the Cardinals.

It took some time, but the Cardinals built a strong team. After winning the 1926 World Series, the team's owner traded Rogers Hornsby for second baseman Frankie Frisch. Starting in 1928, the Cardinals won four of the next seven **NL pennants**.

Players such as Ripper Collins, Pepper Martin, and brothers Dizzy and Daffy Dean helped lead the way to World Series wins in 1931 and 1934.

The 1940s brought more success. Stan Musial was a key figure as St. Louis won four **NL pennants** and three World Series between 1942 and 1946. Musial's batting stance looked odd, but he sprayed line drives all over the field.

GRAND SLAMS

The Cardinals stayed strong in the 1950s and 1960s. Bob Gibson and Lou Brock were stars on the field. The team won the World Series again in 1964 and 1967.

The 1980s brought a new style of play. The Cardinals stole bases, played fast, and won with teamwork. In 1982, they won another World Series title.

28

Mark McGwire made headlines in 1998. He hit 70 home runs that season, setting a new **record** at the time.

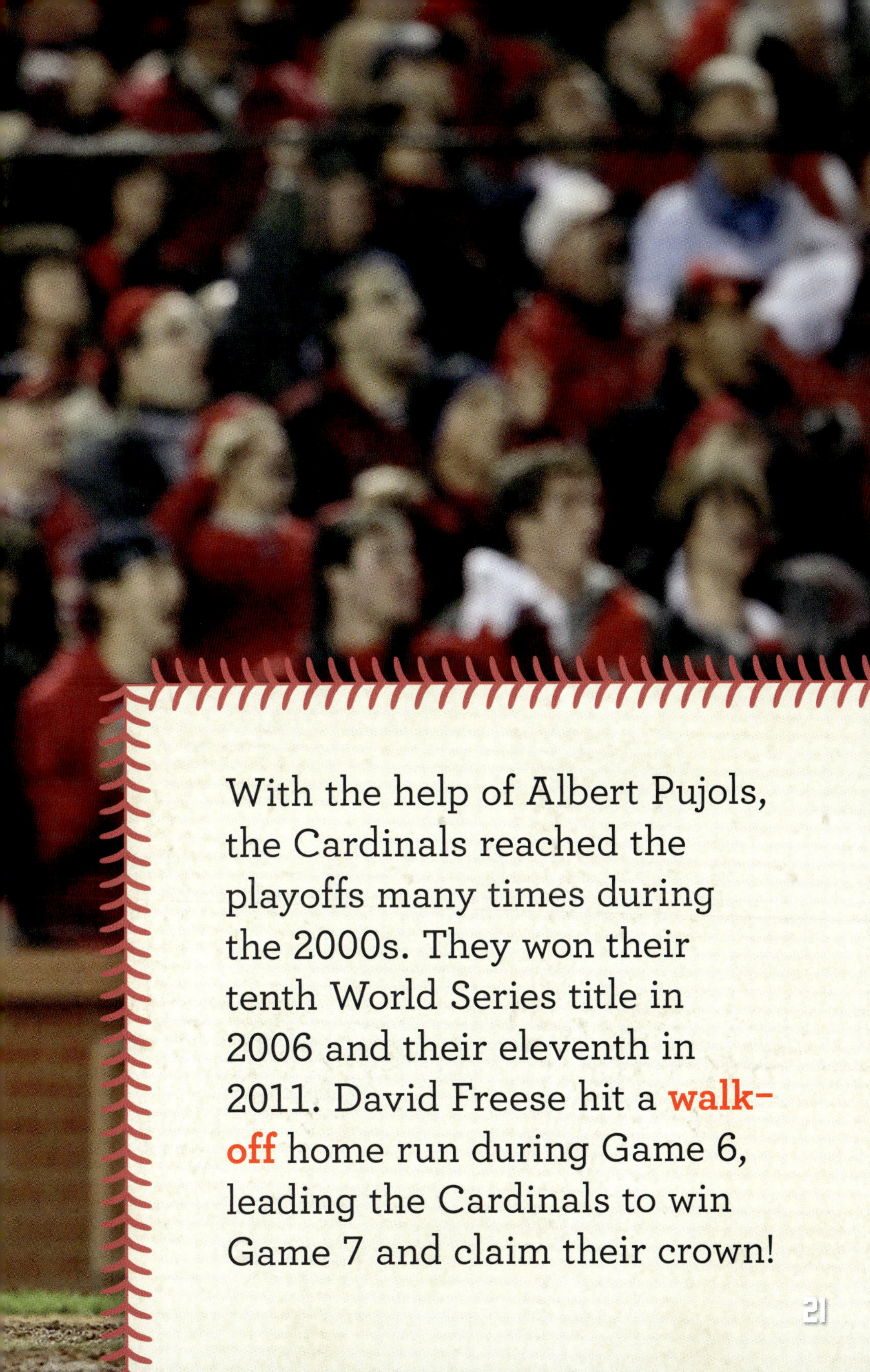

With the help of Albert Pujols, the Cardinals reached the playoffs many times during the 2000s. They won their tenth World Series title in 2006 and their eleventh in 2011. David Freese hit a **walk-off** home run during Game 6, leading the Cardinals to win Game 7 and claim their crown!

From 2012 to 2024, the Cardinals stayed strong, appearing in the **postseason** eight times. They made it to the World Series in 2013 but lost to the Red Sox.

With strong hitting and leadership from players like third baseman Nolan Arenado and catcher Wilson Contreras, the storied St. Louis Cardinals will be back on top soon.

HALL OF FAME

Stan Musial played his whole career with the Cardinals and became one of the best hitters in baseball history. He got 3,630 hits, won seven batting titles, and earned three MVP awards. He helped St. Louis win three World Series. He was **inducted** into the Baseball Hall of Fame in 1969.

Bob Gibson was a fierce pitcher who played his whole career in St. Louis. He won two **Cy Young Awards** and one MVP. In 1968, he had a 1.12 **ERA**, one of the best seasons ever by a pitcher. He helped the Cardinals win two World Series and was named to the Baseball Hall of Fame in 1981.

PUJOLS
5
GEICO
GEICO
GEICO

Albert Pujols hit 469 home runs in a Cardinals uniform. He won three MVP awards and helped the team win the World Series in 2006 and 2011. He also drove in almost 1,400 runs with St. Louis, one of the highest totals in team history. He returned to the Cardinals in 2022 and hit his 700th career home run!

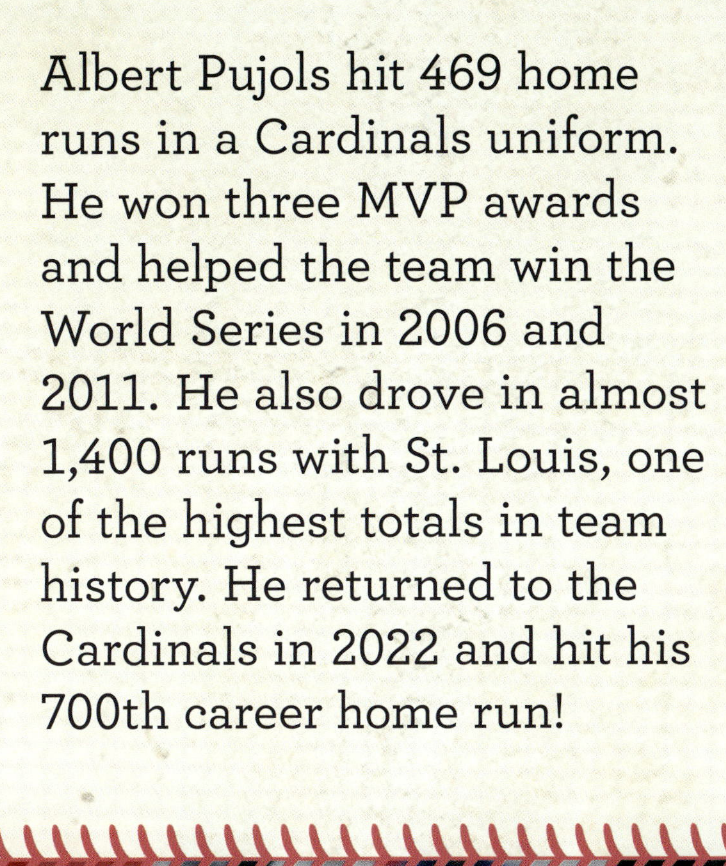

GLOSSARY

Cy Young Award – an annual American baseball award given to the best pitcher in each of the two MLB leagues.

Earned-Run Average (ERA) – the average number of earned runs per game scored against a pitcher.

inducted – brought in as a member.

legacy – the long-lasting impact of particular events that took place in the past.

National League (NL) – one of two 15-team leagues that make up MLB.

pennant – the title achieved by the team that wins its division or league championship.

postseason – the playoffs, including the wild-card round, divisional playoffs, league championship series, and World Series.

record – a top achievement by a team or player that no one has done before.

walk-off – any victory in which the home team scores the winning run in the bottom of the final inning.

ONLINE RESOURCES

To learn more about the St. Louis Cardinals, please visit **abdobooklinks.com** or scan this QR code. These links are routinely monitored and updated to provide the most current information available.

INDEX